Postcard Poets

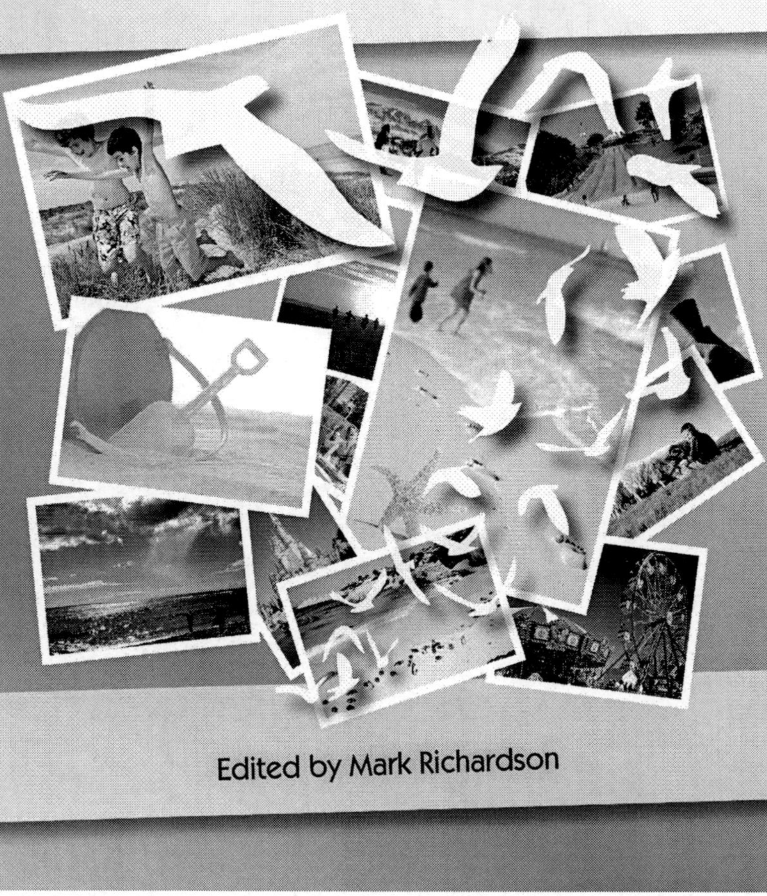

Edited by Mark Richardson

First published in Great Britain in 2011 by:

Young Writers

Young Writers
Remus House
Coltsfoot Drive
Peterborough
PE2 9BF
Telephone: 01733 890066
Website: www.youngwriters.co.uk

Book Design by Neil Daniels

SB ISBN 978-0-85739-666-2

Foreword

Since Young Writers was established we have always endeavoured to promote the joys of reading and writing to children and young adults. Two decades on, we remain just as committed to developing and nurturing the creative talents of the next generation, encouraging them to have a sense of confidence in their own abilities. Seeing their work in print will encourage them to keep writing as they grow and become our poets of tomorrow.

This collection is the result of our latest competition, Postcard Poets, showcasing the best in imaginative poetic talent. The young writers have written in a variety of styles based around the theme of holidays and postcards.

Selecting the poems has been challenging and immensely rewarding. The effort and imagination invested by these young writers makes their poems a pleasure to enjoy reading time and time again.

Contents

The Poems

School's Out

Azure sky,
Summer sun,
School holidays are fun!

Building castles,
On crumbling sand,
Listening to my favourite band!

Eating ice cream,
Creamy and cool,
Jumping in the paddling pool!

Six weeks off,
Feeling free,
No school,
Yippee!

Louise Peacock (11)

All About Sammy

Tasting the gorgeous fish and chips on my tongue.
The crabs waving at the sun.
Hearing the sea stroking the rocks.
Seeing the dolphins jumping out of the sea.
The children paddling in the sea.
Hearing the people enjoying themselves.
Smelling the ice cream.
Tasting the sand on my tongue.
Smelling the sea.

Ethan Jack Hallard (8)

Summer Is Here

Summer is here,
This is the time when adults drink wine and beer,
We go to play in the sea,
With my friends and me.
The sun will shine bright,
Shooting beams of light.
All I can say,
Have a fun day.

I'm eating ice cream,
Having a treasure hunt with my team.
I sleep in my hotel,
While my friends sleep in a motel.
We drink and eat,
Mmm, what a treat.
It's time to go home,
See you next year in Rome.

Kane O'Donoghue Lane (10)

Summer Is Now

Summer is bright,
Bright as light,
Come tonight
And hold on tight.
Play with your kite
And have a good time,
Swim now in the sun,
Buy a bun!

Aleksandra Burnatowska (10)

Bad Holiday

People drink beer,
When they are here,
A few get drunk
And throw up in their bunk!

Sunburn in Spain,
Gives people pain,
It is no fun,
So they put on aftersun.

I know it is bad,
People have to pay,
It drives them mad,
When they have a bad holiday!

Alex Mitchell (10)

Harrison

Soft sand in my socks.
I'm crabbing on the rocks.
Seagulls soaring in the air.
Children running everywhere.
Come along and join the team.
Children running - lots of ice cream.
I buried my hand in the sand.
My dad jumped on the bouncy castle.
I don't know where he'll land.

Harrison Joseph Carey (8)

New Forest Ponies

N ew ponies
E very day
W hinnying in the sun

F oals in fantastic forests
O h what a sight
R ustling through the leaves
E very day and night
S tepping over burrows and
T rotting in delight!

P layful ponies everywhere
O ver the hills, here and there
N ear the rivers
I love to watch them, while
E very night they are in my dreams
S plashing in the silver streams.

Lucy Dryburgh (9)

Disneyland

D umbo is an
I ncredible elephant
S o I love him
N ow I go on the Madhatter's teacups
E veryone is so tiny
Y es
L et's go on the small, old boats
A nd travel around the world
N o one wants to leave
D isneyland.

Matilda Atkinson (6)

Raindrops

R is raindrops speeding down the window like an Olympic sprinter.
A is as the dismal grey clouds roll over our immense house.
I is I gaze out the window miserably.
N is now will a rainbow appear?
D is definitely not.
R is really bored that I am.
O is, 'Oh no!' I cry as the rain pelts down like hailstones.
P is plants hoovering up the water like water being drunk.
S is seeing the rain hurtle down the gutter like the current
of a river.

Shiekinah Ramdeholl (10)

Best Friend For Life

I bumped into my best friend today
She really, really is.
She is my BFFL (best friend for life)
I will not be able to see her at school again
I will miss her
But she will be my BFFL.

Frankie Hemsley (10)

Summer

S ummer is cool,
U nder the hot sun,
M y friends like to play,
M y dogs like lots of extra walks,
E at lots of ice cream,
R un a long way along the beach.

Owen Atkinson (9)

Golden Anniversary

G randma and Grandad
O h, how we love you so!
L et's celebrate,
D on't be shy!
E verybody join in the celebrations!
N o time for relaxing!

A nd so, it's 50 years of marriage . . .
N ot bad when you consider!
N ow we need to say to you,
I n our own special way.
V ery best wishes are sent to you
E ach and every day.
R emember just what you mean to us,
S pecial, loving and kind!
A nd, so to finish off we say
R aise your glass, hip hip hooray!
Y our wonderfully gorgeous grandchildren wish you much love today!

Amelia McKenzie (8)

Boring School

It feels so good to be off school.
Instead of maths, bathing in the pool.
Instead of A, B, C, watching TV,
Dick and Dom specials on CBBC.
I like art because it's good for the heart
And I like to go to the park
But it is rather dark.
Haven't I mentioned I am looking after a fish?
Excuse me while I feed him . . . his dish.

Jess Forbes (8)

Summertime Is Here

Summertime is here,
We're all having fun.
Hope you'll have a nice time
And enjoy each and every day.

I'm going to the beach
To pass my time, it'll be fun.
I'll be playing in the sand
And having lots and lots of fun.

Now holidays are over,
Everyone's coming back from their holidays
And getting ready to go to school
And having loads of fun,
Enjoying literacy and maths.

Sana Anjum (10)

My Time In Devon

Oh I can't wait,
As long as I'm not late.
I have a nice time,
With a wind chime.
Suddenly it is time to go,
I just say no!

We are getting in the car,
Hoping it is not far.
Finally we are at home,
Not just me all alone.
Me with my mum and dad,
All the joy we had.
I wake up and get up,
Then I drink from my cup.
My time in Devon.

Sarah Holcroft (10)

My Summery Fun

In my summer fun I had my tenth birthday,
It was fab and gay in every way,
I rode my brand new bike,
It sparkled like the shimmering sea,
I picked fruit at Hewitts Farm,
Oh what a lovely place to be,
It is the kingdom of fruit,
Bewl Water was a wonderful trip,
I could almost slip,
Chessington was so awesome,
It was like an undiscovered world,
I also did the reading challenge,
I was a bookworm that no one would ever disturb,
I wrote this postcard poem all about my summer,
Writing a poem was the best yet.

Wendy Tu (10)

In July

Let's find a shady, wady, pretty little brook,
Let's have candy and a picture book.
There all day we'll stay and play
And never mind the heat
While the water's screaming
Ripples round our feet.
And we'll gather curly mussel shells while bright,
Frightened minnows darting,
Scurry out of sight.
What if, what if, heighho! My oh!
All the ifs were true
And the fishes wishes,
Now what would you do?

Jak Fishwick (8)

Sunshine In The Air!

The sun is in the air,
Finally summer's here.
I'm free to do whatever I want,
As I smell the lovely scent
Of an ice cream cone.
I relax on a warm, comfy chair.
The sun dazzles my eyes.
I am at the beach.
As I swim as fast as I can
The birds sing a song.
That's all you need.
As the sun begins to rise
I feel the heat.
I would hate to stay inside
When the sun is there.

Temitope Olubanjo (8)

Where Is My Dog?

Where is my dog?
Where is my dog that ran away?
Where is my dog that ran away,
That bumped into a tree?
Where is my dog that ran away,
That bumped into a tree
That had an injury?
Where is my dog that ran away,
That bumped into a tree
That had an injury,
That rolled into the sea?

Sebastian Khosravani Shiri (7)

All About Me

My name is Millie,
I am not so silly,
I have a sister called Maisie,
She is so crazy and lazy
When it comes to getting out of bed,
I have a little brother,
Who is a nutter,
His name is James
And most of the time he is a pain.
I have a mum, Andrea, who is so shouty,
But not all of the time, she's so grouchy.
I have a dad, Chris, who always works
And when he comes home he calls my sister the lurch.

That is my family, we'll never break up
And we'll live happily.

Millie Kirk (8)

My Holiday

M y holiday is as hectic as a hippo
Y ellow as the sun

H appy as a pig in mud
O thers were jealous that our holiday was fun
L icking ice cream was my favourite part
I nteresting day at Poultons Park
D ad got wet on the waterslide
A ltogether we had a photo
Y elled out loud, cheese!

Zachary Woodcock (8)

Monk Park Farm

Today I'm off to Monk Park Farm,
To get up early I set my alarm.
I put on my leggings and my top too,
I'm really going to see the cows that moo.
The guinea pigs are small and cute,
The baby ones are so minute.
The sheep and goats are so mischievous,
They nearly ate my Maltesers.
Before the end I got an ice lolly,
But then we had to get the brolly.
But the rain really did no harm,
Because I still had an amazing day at Monk Park Farm.

Rhianna Bunn (9)

Summer Fun

School's out for summer,
Get the deckchairs out,
Let the kids have fun in the pool
While the men use their tools,
Get a tan,
But you might need a fan,
Stay safe, have some faith
And don't forget that in the sun
You must have fun
'Cause soon it will all come to an end
And it's back to school mums will send.

Alexandra Worboys (10)

Capital FM Rules!

C ool music just for partying
A dults and children enjoy listening to it
P arties will be outstanding with Capital FM
I can't resist singing along
T op artists on nonstop
A ddictive songs can't stop singing to
L aughs are guaranteed

F amily favourites playing 24/7
M illions of prizes to be won

R emixes are on in the evening
U pdated music, never old
L ive music or not Capital FM will blow you away
E ntertainment for everyone
S uitable music for everyone.

Gurneer Flora (10)

Summer Holiday

My holiday was fun and brill,
The sun was shining, without a chill,
We woke in the morning to the countryside
And went to a restaurant and look at the food I tried!
In the pool it was fun and definitely cool,
With splashing the main source of fun,
Especially with that burning sun!
At the beach the waves hit my feet,
Along with everybody that I meet!
My summer was great, can't wait for another,
But first I must look after my brother!

Emily Axten (10)

My Summer Holiday

First I went to Lightwater Valley,
It was very jolly.
It wasn't raining,
So I didn't need my brolly.

Next I went to Killhope,
The mine gave us a fright.
It was very dark,
Because there was not much light.

Then I went to Grandma's,
We went to lots of different places.
When we were finished,
We all had smiley faces.

That's what I did in the holidays,
I hope that next year will be really good again.

Eve Lodge (9)

Summertime

Summertime's wonderful,
Licking luscious ice creams, as the sun beams.

Summertime's amazing,
Beachballs bouncing, as children are pouncing.

Summertime's beautiful,
Flying colourful kites, itching from insect bites.

Summertime's crazy,
Eating fish and chips, whilst drinking lemonade, sips.

Summertime's wonderful,
Catching boat rides, as birds glide.

Hannah Prouse (11)

My Holiday Wedding

The wedding was good,
The hols were great,
My mum ate all the wedding cake,
It was round,
She fell to the ground,
Which made her find a golden pound,
But we didn't like the sound
Of her hitting the hard ground.
Her hubby looked like a hound,
As he was running around the golden pound.

He was fat, he was small,
He was kissing them all,
They fled through the night,
As they saw a terrible fright
Coming into their sight.

Ellie Jones (9)

My Holiday!

Now all my work is done!
And the summer has just begun.
I'm going down to the beach,
To admire the sun,
All my friends are there
And the breeze of fresh air
Is drifting through my hair,
As we all shout, 'Yeah.'

Emily Hurst (9)

Summertime!

My summer was great
One reason because I saw my mate!
We played with my water gun,
It was so much fun!
Some days it rained which was a pain
I went to my grandad's
Who has a dog who is mad . . .
I went on the Wii
And created my own MII.
I watched 'Horrid Histories',
It was a mystery.
We went on a trip
I loved every bit!
I had an ice cream
It made me scream.
What a cool summer.

Louis Cornwall (10)

School's Out!

No more lessons,
No more school,
No more following lots of rules,
We broke up from school today,
Time for fun and time for play.
Cricket, picnics in the sun,
Treasure hunts and lots of fun.
Camping and cooking without a stove,
Going to a beach and exploring a cove.
Rock pools, seashells, bodyboarding in the sea,
Lots of ice creams all for me!

Georgia Alix Thomas (8)

The Seaside

Bobbing, bobbing, bobbing boats,
Waves going crash,
I love going to the seaside with all my family
And Rover too, our pet dog.
There's Grandma's feet getting pinched by crabs,
Grandpa in a deep, deep dream,
Suddenly waking up by Rover licking him.
Dad's doughnut going missing,
With seagulls guzzling Dad's food down.
Mum trying to help Andy swim,
But he keeps crying
And me, I am eating.
Hey! Where did my sandwiches go?
Greedy seagull!

Joshua Williams (10)

Sickle Cell

A sickle is for cutting
Cells join us together
Some days my sickle cells are hurting
It can depend on the weather
I have to sit by the heating to keep warm
My mother talks about beating
But she knows so don't perform
My future is to be an air hostess
But I must stay on ground
You can't be the hostess
With the mostess when your sickle cell
Shakes and grumbles in your limbs.

Renee Gabriel-Whyte (9)

I Love The Seaside

I n the summer I went to the seaside.

L ots of time to play.
O n the sand I'll raise my hands.
V ery sweet ice cream in the van.
E very day it's very hot.

T he sun is so bright it shines in your eyes.
H ats protect our head in the sun.
E vening is soon here.

S ummer is the best time on the beach
E xciting days on the beach.
A nyone can swim on the beach.
S easide cafe is the best.
I ce cream is so tasty.
D resses are allowed on the beach.
E veryone likes the seaside.

Suhayma Ali (7)

Summer Holidays

One hot summer's day
Ice creams and drinks
What really cool links.

We sit in the breeze
That comes from the trees.

In our summer holidays
All we do is stay out and play.

We look forward for the gifts, daytrips too,
We do this in Ramadan, what about you?

Tahseen Al-Zahra (8)

School Days

Today I am at school
But I have been acting like a fool.
My teacher said no and I said ow.
I had a hiccup, always ready to clear up.
It always gets out of hand
When my teacher bellows at me to stand.
Every time I laugh my teacher says get on with your graph.
Pencils start to rustle
And I start to fuss all.
Some people tend to lie
And I ask them why.
I am going to Year 5 and the time is flying by.
It's time to say goodbye.

Isabella Elliott (9)

Summer Poem

Summer poems are so fun,
You can easily get it done.
All you have to do is think,
Or write with the colour pink!
Why don't you play in the sun,
With friends around you that are fun.
When I always play,
I think it's another day.

On the next day I'm going to fly up high
And write in the sky
Bye-bye!

Uzma Khan (9)

At The Seaside

The seaside is a great place to be,
With sparkling shells and big palm trees.
The children jumping and playing in the sea,
What a sight that is to see.
Donkey racing on the beach,
Ice creams waiting for our treat.
Now it's time to say goodbye,
Home to dream of the day gone by!

Tilly Bond (10)

A Nice Summer's Day

Summer is so nice and hot,
That is why I like it a lot.
I think that the summer is great,
Especially when I'm with my mate.
I love going to the park,
Because it's really light in the summer
And not that dark.

Vaneesa Patel (8)

Sun, Sun On The Wall

Sun, sun on the wall,
He is the mightiest of them all.
Sun, sun on the wall,
Your heat will never fall.
Sun, sun is so tall,
Higher than a fish and chips stall.

Josh Rowlinson (10)

Summer's Coming!

Summer's coming, let's all cheer,
Friends and family, they're all here.
Picnics, parks, no more fear,
Come on everyone let's all cheer.

Fairs and rides, let's have fun,
We can all enjoy in the sun.
Beaches, pebbles, shells, let's all enjoy,
Go to Blackpool and buy a toy.

Roses, daffodils and bluebells,
Sunflowers, blue tits and cockle shells.
Everyone happy, loads of smiles.
I missed the shot whilst playing golf,
Don't matter, we could have loads of trials.

Rukhsar Dar (10)

Dear Teacher

As the final bell was rung
We all ran out to have some fun.
Six weeks of holiday,
No homework just lots of play.
My alarm will not be set,
School rules will not be met.
No maths work, no literacy,
Me and my friends will just be free.
Rainy days or summer shine,
We will all be feeling fine.
We'll go for strolls on golden beaches,
While up above the seagull screeches.
Licking lemon tops with flakes,
Perfect picnics with creamy cakes.
I hope that you're relaxing too,
As we are not really missing you.

Daniel Conaghan (11)

Untitled

I am going on holiday
Lots to do
Lots to play!

On the 23rd
I saw a bird
It's fun
Lots to be done!

Starfish
Food's delish!
My mum's gonna text
I'm coming next
I love summer.

Mia Prince-Kelly (7)

Sun, Sun

Sun, sun it is out again
What a sunny day it is
All of the children are playing out again with ice creams
Shining like a big star.

Philip Prince (9)

Bedtime

It's time for bed so what do we do?
We brush our teeth and wash our face,
We give our mum and our siblings a great big kiss,
Then Mum comes and tells us a tale,
Then we can sleep easy.

Sian Welch (10)

Summer Holiday Fun

S wimming is top of your list for you hol!
U p, up, up you're on your way to sun, sun, sun,
M aybe have a little snack before jetting off!
M *unch, crunch, mmm!*
E rr, which luxury pool first,
R ing family, send postcards (got to do!)

H ot, lovely, boiling sun which give me a tan.
O nly fun is allowed
L ie and just relax.
I ce cream, smell the ice cream.
D ay naps so that means later bedtime!
A qua blue sea,
Y ummy ice cream

F un activities
U nder the sun, hearing the splashing sea
N ow what is your dream holiday?

Mia Smith (10)

Summertime

A whale lives under the sea
While we are playing free.
I like to play outside
When it's cosy and dry,
Going to the beach is fun
And trying new things will be done.
This is a season called summer,
Which will make you dumber.
Everyone will go to a new year,
Soon it will be quite near.

Fariha Chowdhury (8)

My Summer Holiday

I've been round my grandma's,
It was very sunny,
We played some silly games,
It was really funny!
We also went to Suffolk,
To see my aunt and nan,
We put some music on to dance,
So we did the cancan!
Then we went on a boat,
To sail to lovely Holland,
I want to go again,
So I need a magical wand.
Well, that's the end of our holiday,
We had great fun,
Now I'm really tired,
From playing in the sun.

Katie Bennett (10)

My Garden

My garden is a lovely spot,
Where I sunbathe when it's hot,
Since I was a tot, a tot,
Cool or hot never mind the weather,
Even when I find a feather,
I love my garden,
Since I was a tot, a tot,
Yeah I love my garden,
Since I was a tot.

Emily Hunter (10)

Going On A Holiday

Leaving home,
Leaving the rain,
I'm going on an aeroplane.

Cases packed,
Passports out,
It's holiday time,
Let's jump and shout.

Arrive at airport,
Long delay,
Dad snoring,
It's so boring.

Flight is called,
We're on our way,
We're going on a holiday.

Swimming pool,
Suntan cream,
Holidays are such a dream.

Jasmine Scott (11)

Summer Fun

Rain isn't funny, please be sunny,
I like summer, you like winter,
Summer holidays are nearly here.

Plants and trees are growing strong,
Insects flying on and on.

Rainbows bright with pots of gold,
Soon the weather will be cold.

The sun is bright whilst shining its rays,
While I'm enjoying my school holidays.

Abbie Darley (10)

I'm On Holiday

I'm on holiday,
Six weeks' holiday,
Lots of time to play,
Six weeks' holiday.

We all go to LegoLand,
Then to the seaside,
Play on the sand.

Scooting in the fresh air,
Having fun without a care.

Watching daytime TV,
No school, I'm free.
Hooray! Hooray!
Yippee!

Joseph Lennon Furnell (11)

Summer Days

Lazy days,
Happy days,
Beach days,
Friend days,
Walking days,
Biking days,
Singing days,
Dancing days,
Windy days,
Rainy days,
Cloudy days,
Sunny days,
Holidays,
Holidays,
Six weeks
Holidays!

Aiden Paul Purvis (11)

Harry's Hobbies

We go to our caravan
It is by the sea, we catch some crabs
And have a swim, my brother Tom and me.

When it rains it changes things,
Inside I have to be, then I play
Computer games on my Wii.

I get on the train to London
With my brother and my mum.
We have a really lovely time
And sometimes we let Dad come.

There are lots of things that I really like to do
I play football for my team
But to play at Wembley is my real dream.

Harry Robinson (6)

About Summer

Summer is lovely like a flower.
Come with me and you will see
What summer means to me.
The sun is shining in the sky
Saying hello to those who fly,
Also people walking by,
People mowing the grass all day
Until their backs all give way.
On the beach we like to play
Netball and build sandcastles, what a day!
Jelly and ice cream, what a treat,
Not all the time it rots your teeth.
In the summer I'm going to Gran's.
I might see Maisie one of my friends.
I haven't seen her in ages,
She's also my penpal friend.

Angel May Egan (8)

I Can See A Rainbow

I can see a rainbow, way up in the sky.
See the range of colours, just slightly out of my eye.
A mix of rain and sun.
This is what I see when I'm having so much fun!
You watch the rainbow shine and wonder where it ends.
Me and my friends have so much fun, under all the summer sun.
Then a rainbow appears again - you see it brightly shine,
Then you wonder why it's here this time?

Callum Mortlock (10)

Summer - Haiku

Summer is so great,
I like eating sausages,
I love summer now.

Maygen Lockham (9)

Summer Holidays

S ummer is full of fun,
E specially in sunny weather,
A t school we learn all day,
S ometimes I dream
I had an ice cream
D ad's car broke down
E nglish, maths, come back again!

Lewis Shaw (9)

Seaside Fun

The waves crash against the shore.
We watch. We listen.
No hesitation. Diving, jumping, swimming,
Even bodyboarding.

Sandcastles have been built
But always falling.
Waves coming fast, everyone running.
Hurrying. Pushing. No one staying.

People enjoyed that.
End of a great day out.

The beach's waiting for your next day out
At your nearest beach.

Hettie Marlene Elizabeth Cook (11)

Sun Shining, Sun Cream

The sun shines brightly on my face
As my mum splashes me in sun cream,
The sound of bright yellow sand being sprinkled
Around by my brothers,
Splashes of water from water gun's going everywhere,
People laughing, people crying,
Plastic swords clashing, suddenly splatters of rain hitting the ground
Like cannonballs invading,
My suncream drips slowly off my body, I look around,
Everybody's shouting and running into my large and gorgeous house.
I am outside on my own, the doors are locked,
I'm cold . . .

Katelyn Dodd (10)

Summer World

In the garden there's flowers, they look like showers.
Skies are white, the sun is bright.
The world is light.
The world has a height.
Summer's coming, holidays start so be a part of summer.
Times come and go, but summer wouldn't go.
World is hot but not thicker than a pot.
I am going to Holland to see summer, real summer.
Hotness, coldness, all counts in summer,
Sunshine is orange but mixed with yellow,
That gives a bright sight of life,
Summer is beautiful,
Summer is historical.

Hadia Quimmi (9)

I Love Summer

I love summer

L ove the scented flowers
O ranges are sweet
V egetables are ripe
E very person is smiling

S ummer sun
U nique art is flowing
M orning, evening and night
M y life is full of fun
E ating lush strawberries
R oses grow taller.

Chelsea Louise Margaret Stimpson-Thurlby (10)

It's Summertime Again

It's a great day so I go outside to play
Because it's a fun day!
I go to the seaside
I see what I'll find.
I never know what I'll find.
Maybe I will see someone I know.
I listen to the birds twitter and have fun,
I can feel the warmth of the sun;
I hear kids playing and laughing in the street.
I am in the park;
Having lots of fun with my friends
'Cause it's a hot, hot summer's day
So I enjoy the summer a lot!
Summer's the best of all weathers!

Faith Ako (10)

The Sea

I arrive at the beach, I hear the cry of a seagull, harsh and loud.
The yelps of excited dogs as their owners throw them Frisbees.
I walk to the edge of the vast blue ocean,
The waves make a slapping against the sand,
Loud but rather calming.
At long last I climb onto the barnacle-encrusted wall
and dive; dive into the cool water so I cannot hear the seagulls,
The dogs or the waves, just a soft swishing as I dive deeper and deeper.
I have to go back but I will spend most of my time here,
It's my place, it's where I should be.
The sea.

Julia Imogen Walker Ransom (10)

Untitled

Things on sunny days, fishing, trampolines,
Fun outside, playing in the sun.
British rainy days are so grim stuck in the house,
Staying in Blery's,
A trip to Paignton Zoo,
Where we spent a happy year or two.
We had so much fun,
Looking at the animals with my mum.
Running round playing tag with brother and sisters,
Oh what a drag.
On grotty days with rain a-pouring,
Xbox 360 games we were playing,
But so soon, holiday over,
Back to school,
Ends out days of clover.

Thomas Devine (10)

Summertime Fun

Summertime is fun
Now it has begun
Birds are cheeping
Frogs are leaping
Bees collecting
Children reflecting
On what they have done
During their summertime fun.

Kiera Shaughnessy (10)

Holiday Heaven

I'm on holiday - hooray! At last!
I'm down at the seaside, slapping on suncream, fast!
I drank a strawberry smoothie,
As the sun shone above me.
Then I swam in the pool and ate ice cream,
I got my shades
And my buckets and spades.
As I stood in front of the sea,
I could feel the warm sand as it crept through my toes,
And I loved watching the sun set,
Down it goes!

Amal Yusuf (10)

My Summer Holiday

I am going to Haven,
It's going to be fun,
I'm going to get sunburnt
In the hot and blazing sun.
I will play in the pool,
The weather will be cool.
I will be eating lots of sweets
While my brother stares and drools.
My brother and I will argue
While my mum puts on a barbecue.
In the night I will go to the arcade
And play for a decade!

Frazer Muluaney (8)

Rolling Down A Hill!

I'm rolling, rolling, rolling down,
I'm rolling down a hill.
I'm rolling, rolling, rolling down,
I'm rolling down it still!
I'm rolling, rolling, rolling down,
I'm rolling down a hill.
I'm rolling, rolling down,
But now I'm feeling ill!

Naomi Meddon Schelvis (9)

Summer Poem

I wake up in the morning
And I see the sun shining
By the blue sky.
I go to the park,
I hear the birds tweeting
And the babies crying.
I go home and pack my things
And I get on a plane
And soon the summer holiday is over.
Summertime is the best
Better than all the rest,
Hooray!

Khadija Begum (10)

Holidays

Holidays are fun,
Holidays are great.
This holiday I am going to France,
I'm so excited it makes me want to dance.

Holidays are fun,
Holidays are great.
My cousins are coming to stay,
They make me laugh with joy when we play.

Holidays are fun,
Holidays are great.
My friends might be coming round,
They make me not want to stop playing
And all you hear is a jolly sound.

I love holidays!

Katie Thompson (9)

Summer

A poem about the summer is all you need to do,
So don't be lazy and play out
While the sun is shining bright,
The sky is very blue,
I'm going on my holidays where it's very hot,
The plane will last over night,
I hope my brother is coming - not!
When we're there we may fight,
There'll be waterslides there,
But once I went to Haven,
This time I hope there's a fair,
I wonder if I'll go caving . . .

Rebecca Critchley (8)

The Holiday Has Begun

The school bell has rung,
It's time for fun,
'Cause the holiday has begun.
Camping, skiing, making things too,
Trying to find other things to do.
Taking a ride in an aeroplane,
And then landing in Spain.
Visiting a party in France,
And getting taught how to dance.
Going to visit the Pope,
Then go skiing at the slope.
Go down to the art club,
And then grab a bit of grub.
Stop off at a casino,
And meet a bambino.
Visit the sandy coast,
'Cause I like that the most.
Go back to my house,
And chase a little mouse.
Now it's September,
How wouldn't I remember,
I'm doing something not so cool . . .
I'm having to go back to school!

David Burrows (10)

Summertime

Birds are tweeting,
Summer's beating under the heat.
Lying in the fresh cool pool
Under the heat,
Trying to find some shade
With your lemonade.
Gold sand under your feet,
With the Earth's heavenly beat.
After light the stars shine bright,
After a summer light.
Planting a bulb to make things bright.
One summer's night the moon shines bright.
Skipping all day long with a hula hoop as well.
Fish dancing through the sea.
Because it's really hot suncream comes out the pot.
Hear the choirs in the park
Because the summer's here to park.

Shanté Jackson & Keely Stallard (9)

Beach

We went to the beach today,
Almost got lost on the way!

I splashed about in the sea,
Having fun, just being me.

Playing in the waves was fun,
But how I wish we'd had some summer sun!

Evan Pearce (7)

Give Me The Joys Of Summer

Give me the joys of summer,
Birds flying around in pairs.
Poppies in the meadow,
Bees and butterflies are there.

The garden looks so wonderful,
All the flowers are in full bloom.
Come and join the fairy ball
And wish upon the moon.

Walks on the beach, hunt for shells
And then we'll have an ice cream.
Warm summer nights, we'll play out late,
And have lots and lots of lie-ins!

No school for us, it's time to play,
We'll all have fun together,
Swings, slides, tennis and swimming,
How I wish summer could last forever!

Eleanor Murphy (10)

Romania

I'm going to Romania,
It's not near Saudi Arabia,
They like peach, pears (fruit),
They like animals but they shoot,
They like football not pool,
They like sun not a bun,
They like roads not toads you see,
You can't change them,
They're them,
So there!

William Price (10)

My Summer Poem

On this summer day,
I take part in a fabulous play.
There I have an ice cream,
By the flowing stream.
I kneel down in the sun,
To have a quick bun.
And then I have my tea,
With my uncle and aunty.
Then I play with my friends,
And make up such a cool trend.
I see some fish,
And catch them in a dish.
Next, I play cards
With a few scary guards,
And tuck into cooked lards.
So, this is my feeling of fun
About all the things I've done.

Baamini Sabanathan (10)

The Beach

The sky is blue
The sun is shining
And so are you.
The children are playing
With their buckets and spades
All day through.

Mia Bartram (8)

Sunny Days

Another year of school is done
No more work, it's time for fun
Sunny days, long warm nights,
Twinkling stars, make pretty lights
Happy days, lots of fun, making plans in the sun
The beach is what I like the most
The soft warm sand, between my toes
I love the sea, all calm and blue
To paddle, swim and jump waves too
Holidays, exciting times, aeroplanes or fast train rides
Seeing family, far away, special treats, special days
This is the end of my poem today
I hope you enjoyed what I had to say
The summer is great, the summer is here
The summer for me, is the best time of year!

Katy Kitto (10)

Summertime

Summer is my favourite time of the year
I've come up with this poem so listen with your ear
The sun is shining in the sky
The birds tweet as they fly by
The flowers spread their petals as they grow
All their beautiful colours on show
The sky is clear, not a cloud in sight
The sun blasts its heat with all its might
This is why summer's my favourite part
I love summer with all my heart!

Archie Scrivens (8)

Long Hot Summer!

I'm on my holidays and we're all having fun
We all love playing under the big bright sun,
Sun hats and cream, also lots of ice cream,
We're on the beach, the sand between our toes,
Wearing sunglasses while the sun glows,
With our family we all play happily,
In the cool pool we lie on our floats
While you look at the ocean and all there is are boats,
The smell of fish and chips makes us all lick our lips,
Back to school in September,
All these memories I hope to remember!

I'll miss Year 5 and what we have done,
But I can't wait for Year 6 to come!

Georgia Burrows (10)

The Zoo

In the zoo,
There's tigers, gorillas and a kangaroo,
Be careful of the lions,
They might eat you!

Down at the aquarium,
You can see lots of fish,
Including big ones, small ones
And even jellyfish!

Deep in the Arctic
Where polar bears run,
Where penguins are sliding
And having lots of fun!

Maddie Smith (9)

My Summer Holiday

We went to Ingoldmells,
Where it smells,
Of the newly fresh sea
And burgers for me.

I stopped up late
Because Dad bought some bait,
To catch some fishes,
To serve up some dishes.

We went on the fair rides
And had lots of fun,
A lady in the market
Did my hair in a bun.

We had fun at the sea,
Mum, Dad and me.

Hollie May Hipkiss (10)

Summer

Summer is fun sitting under the sun
It lights the day that has just begun
The sun is shining beautifully
Let's go to the beach you and me
Let's enjoy the summer, day by day
Just before it goes away
Summer is a lovely sight to see
It starts the day beautifully.

Eleanor Lovett (10)

Summer When The Sun Is Bright

The summer when the sun is bright,
Long are days and short is night,
The time when you go out of doors,
Go, play on the moors.

You go to the beach to collect shells,
And to smell those seaside smells,
Go abroad to foreign land,
Land your boat on soft white sand.

Cockerels crowing in the morning,
Sun is out when day is dawning,
You might go to a football club,
Or you might relax at the pub.

Luke Hayward (8)

It's Summer

See the little birdies
Chirping in their nest
The best season is summer
By far it beats the rest
Don't forget the suncream
You're rushing out the door
'I don't want to go Mum,
I've been to the beach before.'
Summer's so fun, it's just that time of year
When all the adults drink their wine and beer
Everybody's running, having such a blast
Come on guys, it's bedtime
They fall asleep at last.

Marley Morgan-Campbell (10)

The Seaside

Ice cream and doughnuts, all things sweet,
This day is one big treat!
The golden sun beams down at the sand,
Seagulls sing like one big band.
The sea swiftly sways in and out,
Little children shouting about.
Boats of all different sizes sail on the sea,
This is the best day there could ever be.

Megan Patchett (10)

School

At the seaside there are sea shells
In churches you can hear the ringing of bells
Why does a dog go woof?
Why do humans huff and puff?
In my class there is Alex the monkey
He can groove and he is funky.

Boring is represented by school.
But just, only just . . . it can sometimes be cool.

Fern Harrison (9)

Waves

Waves that bob like barnacles
Waves that crash against bumpy rickety rocks
Waves that are blue, like the twinkling sky
Wonderful waves every day.

Leaha Bennett (10)

Summertime Fun

Finally summertime is here
School time is over
It's time to play
Come on, let's play
It's summertime fun
Going to the beach
Having a swim
Having ice cream to cool
Sun on my face
Isn't it crazy?
Collecting shells
Is my new hobby
I love listening to the birds
Twittering and fluttering in pairs
I stand beneath the sun
Wrapped in nature's blanket
Looking at the little children
Laughing, crying and playing
Summertime fun is fun.

Idil Shire (9)

Summer Holidays Poem

Sun, sun, I went to France,
Sun, sun, it was too hot,
It was so red,
I need glasses,
Sun, sun, what's your name?
I would like to get to know you.
Bye-bye sun, goodbye.

Esther Simuene (8)

Summer Light

Summer light
Summer night
Summer feels alive and bright

Floating breezes
Fresh and free
Gentle sunkissed bumblebee
Curling creatures sleeping so
Marching ants
They come and go
Tall grass bends in sunlit beams
Birds sing their summer song
All day long
Bluebells dance like woodlands' daughters

Summer light
Summer night
Summer feels alive and bright.

Bobby-Lee Whinney (10)

The Seaside

Sitting by the seaside,
Playing with the sand,
As the waves come in,
It sprinkles out of my hand.

I can hear the seagulls flying up above,
As the waves crash against my toes,
This is the sort of day I love.

I lick my ice cream, lick, lick, lick,
I have to eat it quick, quick, quick,
As it melts down my hand,
I hope I don't drop it on the sand!

Tia Webber (10)

A Summer Holiday

I wake in the morning as the sun welcomes me with a warm welcome hug,
I run off into the park where I hear the natural music of the world,
The birds singing and twittering,
The laughter of children playing in the grass,
It's Mother Nature's choir,
The music of the ice cream truck.
I go on the swings,
I swing as high as I can,
I feel as if I am in space,
I jump off the swings,
I go home,
Pack my bags,
Hooray,
I'm on my way,
On my way to a family retreat!
Hip hip
We've come at last,
Where to go to first?
The pool,
The seaside,
The arcade,
The friendly atmosphere,
I wish I could stay here forever.

Tahmina Hannan (10)

The Rocky Shores

As I wake up to a singing bird,
I get my bags and set off to a wonderful beach,
The seas wave as the sand tumbles into the water!
The ice cream boat sails by onto the shore!
I hoped my day would never end but it had to
So I got an ice cream and got my bags and walked home.
As I was walking I just found out the right time
Which made me turn around for some more fun.

Mia Lane (8)

Five Senses At The Seaside

I can hear happy voices calling,
Seagulls screeching and squawking, diving for fish,
Waves crashing on the beach, rising and falling.
I can see the boats, motors churning,
Sail boats sailing, sails flapping,
Crabs scuttling with angry pincers clicking.
I can smell salty water dripping from my nose,
Hot sun warming the sand.
I can feel gooey seaweed sticking in my toes,
Warm and slipping through my fingers.
I can taste salty water stinging on my tongue,
And crunching in my teeth,
Ice cream, cold and sweet, trickling down my chin.
Touching, smelling, seeing, hearing, tasting:
All five senses make the beach a perfect place to be.

Joe Bruton (8)

Summer

Sun go away, we all want to play,
It is far too hot, like yesterday.

Sweat, we all hate sweat,
Sweating all day with the sun shining above us.

Swimming pool, we love you,
You keep us cool when we are hot,
And fed up of the sun.

Summer is very fun, we get hot,
We stand in the shade and play outside all day.

Tenesha Rowe (9)

Summer On The Beach

There was once a woman
Who went to the beach,
She wore a shiny shirt,
Which looked like a peach.

She had
A cat,
Who wore
A fancy hat.

They played together
On the sand,
Then there came
A rock band.

Then it was time to go home,
The cat groaned.

Sara Isse (9)

One Hot Day

I wake up in the morning
The sun kissing my forehead
I go down to the beach
Watch the children play
Watch the waves wetting the sand
Watching the seagulls going in and out of the water
Hear the birds twittering
The smell is so nice
Toddlers splashing in the warm water
The sun melting everything away.

Asma Mohamed (10)

Untitled

The sky is so blue,
Not a cloud to be seen.
The earth is a painting
With every shade of green.
The chirping of birds
As they gracefully fly by,
Amidst the golden hue
Of the lustrous sky.

The flowers are so fragrant,
The trees are their shield,
For under the scorching heat
A breeze they should feel.
The voices of children,
As they play in the park.
It is a definite sign,
Summer has made its mark.

Andrew Geo Johnson (8)

As The Seaweed Swayed

As the seaweed swayed dolphins curl in,
Sharks nibbled on it,
The sea horses hide as they play hide-and-seek.
Seals play in the swaying seaweed,
As the seaweed swayed a rough wave got in,
Seashells went in and the seaweed stopped suddenly.
The animals went out sad
And the seaweed died and all that was left
Was a small pretty stone!

Saffron Grace Green (8)

Someone Belongs To You

Children playing outside
Having lots of fun
Going to the Ukraine
Having loads of fun
People are leaving
And people are crying
But it's not lots of fun
We have to revise
Or the teachers will burst
When the teachers will burst
We will burst
People are coming back
People are happy
There's one way to say we're happy
I'm sorry to say summer is over
Go back to school
And like your new classes.

Calab Nartey (8)

Summer Days

Summer days are great
I get to stay up late
I like to play with friends
The fun just never ends
Picnics in parks and baking cakes
Bike rides, cinema and holidays at the lakes
I love it at the seaside
Jumping the waves, a donkey ride
Climbing trees, playing on the Wii
Having a pizza for my tea.

Nancy Allan (7)

Summer

Summer is so lovely,
But sometimes quite badly,
The sun behaves often,
I am going to the beach,
Where my tutor will teach,
Until I say leach,
Which isn't even a word,
I am at the beach starting to swim,
When I met a boy called Tim,
He ran over to the beach and said,
'I want to get eaten by the shark,'
And so he did,
I couldn't believe my eyes,
Because he always said lies,
As soon as I met him,
That's what he said, that he was wearing a few ties,
Which wasn't even true.

Prathisan Ketheeswaran (9)

Summer, Summer

Summer, summer, we all love it,
We go on holiday, that's the best ever,
Lovely sunshine, sunny and bright,
Makes me happy, funny with delight.

Lots of adventures to enjoy,
Lots of friends to be found
To find shells on the ground
Oh summer, summer
We love you!

Chloe Stokes (9)

Summer Camping

Here we are, almost there,
Sun and flowers everywhere.
Unpack your suitcase and help with the tent,
Be careful with the pegs
Because they might get bent.
Hop in the pool and have a good time,
You and your family are feeling fine.
Hop into bed now it's been a good day,
You look very tired so you had better hit the hay!
It's been a lovely day
And I'd better get to bed,
We're going hiking tomorrow
And there's a whole week ahead!

Have a good summer holiday!

Katherine McCollum (9)

Ready For The Summer

Little Lucy Sanders comes home from school,
Ready for the holidays and the paddling pool.
Her elder sister, Margaret, wants to get a tan,
She sits in a deckchair waving a purple fan.
Matthew and young Joshua have some water balls,
They throw them at the windows and the bumpy walls.
Mum sips a cocktail, looking very fine,
While Dad sneakily opens a bottle of expensive wine.
The holidays have come and now it's time
To have a little fun and let everything hang loose!

Evie Simpson (11)

Summertime!

It's summertime, hip, hip hooray!
I wonder what I should do today.
Go outside, splash in the pool
Have an ice cream so I'll feel cool.
Sunny days are the best days
Going to the park is better.
Birds in birdbaths, dipping in and out
Go to the beach and shout
Having vacations in hotels and villas
This is great, I do feel swell!
Open the windows, get a breeze
The sun is so hot no one will freeze!
Fans turned on, blowing your hair,
Summertime is here and I really do care.

Jasmine Alakija (10)

The Beach

Golden warm sand suffocated my body,
Seagulls' cries opened people's eyes,
From their sleep in the scorching sun.

Ubiquitous waves echoed through caves,
Causing the cliffs to tremble with delight,
The turquoise sea indulged my body,
Making me feel free!

Marcus Davies (10)

Something Special

In my summer holiday,
I dreamt up some mind mixers
Of why oceans are blue,
And why adults are tall and children are small,
Why the world takes twenty four hours to spin on its axis,
Why balls are bouncy,
Why grass is green,
Why people think pink is for girls and blue is for boys
Or why do you think different from me,
Why, why, why, why,
Can all of this be?
Try to think of the answers to these mind mysteries.

Annie Griffin (10)

Nature Calls

The icy winds go by
As the skylarks scream in the sky
Rain draws near
With hares and deer
No man ever comes here.

Green silk leaves rip
The ocean sings
The ocean wave
And soon comes the snow of death
Nature's calling.

Emily Tennick (10)

My Spain Poem

S o hot
U sually playing all day
N ever cold
N ever boring
Y ou always have fun

S uch nice weather
P lenty of sun
A lways sunny
I n Spain you have the most fun ever
N ice beaches.

Amber Bird (9)

In The Sunny Weather

Today was a horrid day
My friend Jake could not play
He was out being a Scout
In the sunny weather.

Today was a good day
My friend Jessica came to play
We played out and about
In the sunny weather.

Amelia Foster (9)

Untitled

S oft sand in-between your toes on the beach
U nder the sun umbrella when it's sunny
M eeting new friends on holiday
M alibu is the perfect break for you
E ating your favourite meal
R oasting hot as you play on the beach.

F un in the sun as you have a holiday break
U nder the sea, doing some snorkling
N ow everybody's having fun!

I n the hotel room chilling
N othing makes your break any better than this.

S unscreen is what you put on so don't you get sunburnt
U nder the bed covers all cosy and warm
N ow the break's over, time to go back to England!

India Jones (10)

Summer Days

Now has come the summer, the middle of the year,
The world has started brightening, so give summer a cheer.
Roses in the flowerbed, daisies in the field,
Birds are singing sweetly, for all the world to hear.
Golden rays of sun, shining from the sky,
Lighting up the daytime, to winter say goodbye.

Hannah Cameron (10)

Summer Is . . .

Summer is waves crashing against the wall,
Summer is lying down in the sun,
Summer is resting in my bed,
Summer is seagulls doing tricks in the air,
Summer is ice cream melting on my toes,
Summer is the time we have some fun!

Jake Scott (7)

Cats And Dogs

Cats and dogs go round the streets
Dogs chase their tails
Cats climb up trees
It's always fun to run and play
With cats and dogs on a sunny summer's day.

William Foster (6)

Summer Fun!

Look, look, the sun is in the sky,
Look, look, there's a butterfly,
Look, look, I'm on the beach,
Look, look, the tide is out of reach,
Now run, it's so fun,
Cornwall is the place to come!

Catherine Old (8)

Hush The Silence

Hush the silence begins
The birds start tweeting
Bees flying around
Hush the silence begins

Shh the quietness
As the flowers start to grow
The whispers in the wind of the trees
Shh the quietness

Hush the silence begins
The birds start tweeting
Bees flying around
Hush the silence begins
Hush!

Jessica Moore (11)

Jolly Holiday

Oh, look at the bright, bright sun
In this weather you're most likely to have fun
Watch your mum make food from a sizzling pan
Or race to the ice cream van
Can you resist the smell of the sea?
Well, neither can we.

Go to the plane, wear something bright not plain
Tell people to shift when you want to see a crane lift
Or read a book
And take one more look.

Fiona Zeka (8)

Down By The Seaside

Down by the seaside,
Fish and chips for tea,
The thought of greasy fingers,
Is filling me with glee.

Down by the seaside,
There's lots and lots to see,
Amusements on the pier,
Fun for you and me!

Down by the seaside,
Paddling in the sea,
Jumping over stones and shells,
One, two, three!

Emily Little (10)

Bestival

Today I'm going to Bestival.
I cannot wait a bit.
There's knitting tents and everything.

There's things you can see
Like the circus stuff,
There's somewhere you can go and camp,
I like the sound of that.
There's a playground and all,
It just sounds great.

Jessica Currie (8)

At The Seaside

At the seaside the sun shines on me
Ahh, how I love the warmness of the breeze
When you go into the sea you might be surprised at what you can see.
When you are boiling hot there is one thing you do,
It is to get an ice cream that will suit you.
When people are grilling food they might be far away
But you can smell the food from a mile away.
If you have a little sister she might just bury you in the sand,
It will be fun at first then you will get cramps and it will hurt.
I love the seaside, the adventures you can go on
And the things you may find.
Ahh, sun, I have enjoyed the time we spent,
I hope I will see you again, goodbye for now,
I can't wait until next time.

Jade Miller (10)

The Summer Holidays

I love the summer days and the smell of ice cream
Just makes me faint, in Cyprus where I am
You're playing in hot sand that's white and gold
And I love looking into the nice blue sky
While the sun's heat sweats you to death
Birds flapping their wings with lovely noises
Going on vacation in a luxury hotel
Where swimming pools are there to relax you
Plus your own room with windows open
And the wind just cools you like an ice pole
In the park where it's wide all you do is walk
On the grass where you can only feel wind
And the sun shines on you every day.

Barry Chimonides (9)

Disneyland Paris

D isneyland here I come
I n the middle of the sun
S eeing Mickey Mouse and all of his other
N ice friends
E very day the joy can't end.
Y ou will want to book your days here.
L eaving Disneyland will make me sad
A nd coming back will make me glad.
N ever, ever have I been somewhere like it
D isneyland, you're so great

P erhaps someday soon me
A nd my family will
R eturn for more fun.
I love Disneyland Paris
S o roll on 28th August 2011.

Ellie Clarke-Deering (10)

Did You Know . . .

Did you know that a butterfly can fly?
Did you know that a fish could die?

Did you know that frogs can leap?
Did you know that moles can dig deep?

But it doesn't matter,
Even if you include the Hatter.

Molly O'Donnell (10)

My Super Summer

In the summer I'll be a year older,
Being ten will make me much bolder.
Scoffing my face with cake all day,
'I'm going to explode!' that's what I'll say.

Then I'll be on my way to France,
Eating frogs' legs if I'm given the chance.
Euro Disney is the place where I'll be,
And Mickey is the person my brother wants to see.

When I get back I'll be in London,
Sightseeing with my uncle, I'll have so much fun.
Then I'll be dreading to come back to school,
Walking halfway around the school again is not so cool.

Tadiwa Sarah Jamera (9)

About My Summer

A poem about my summer,
Is what you're wanting me to write,
So here it goes, it might not be right.
Having a party with all my chums,
Wondering what it will be like when tomorrow comes.
Splashing around in my pool,
Falling down my water wall,
What a great time we are going to have,
I never want this poem to end.

Samantha Hilbery (11)

Summer

On a summer's day
Go to your friends and play.
Have fun in the sun
Until the day is done.
With buzzy bees all round
And worms underground.
We got out the pool
And acted a fool.
We picked a flower
And had more power.
At the end of the day
We went our own way.

Ellie Phillipson (9)

Camping

My pillow's very damp,
My feet are sopping wet,
Mum promised lots of fun
But I haven't found it yet.

The field's turned to mud,
My wellies filled with rain,
All we eat is beans on toast,
I wish we went to Spain.

But then the sun comes out
And I've made loads of friends,
Camping is just brilliant,
I wish it wouldn't end.

Issy Hatch (10)

A Day At The Seaside

'Jump in the car,' said Mum and Dad,
We are off to the seaside today,
We'll sing our songs and laugh a lot,
Feeling excited to be on our way.

After a while we arrived at the beach,
Gathering our buckets, spades and our balls,
The sand was hot, the sun was bright,
But the sea was the best of all.

We rode a donkey and ate ice cream and chips,
Made sandcastles and swam in the sea,
We played at the amusements and had so much fun,
What a day, I'm as happy as can be.

Bailey Heyes (10)

The Sea

As the varnished pebble is thrown into the water,
Golden ripples appear like mountains.
The pebble however slowly sinks down into the deep blue sea,
Waiting to be discovered or maybe never to be seen again.

At sunset the sun goes down,
And the moon, like a mirror on the shining face of the sea,
Comes up and welcomes the nightlife of the sea.
At midnight, the life of the sea disappears,
The waves like white silver horses,
Gallop onto the golden shore, full of shining sand.
The school of fish go to sleep and tomorrow is another day.
And when the world awakes they will celebrate the new day.

Rachel Jackson & Charlotte Baker (10)

Seaside Poem

In my summer I will be,
diving right under the sea.

Eating ice cream all day long,
room for fish and chips, yum, yum, yum.

Sandcastle competition, I'll beat you,
until the tide comes in with the water so blue.

Peasholme Park, such a delight,
I fell in the water once, what a fright.

At the end of summer I will be
waiting for the horror that awaits me.

Trinity Catch (10)

Summer

The summer is hot and full of delight,
The sky is clear, what can I hear . . .
Birds are singing, children laughing with joy, bees humming,
Days seem endless, nights are short.
The sun is so bright as it glows in the sky,
Flowers are in full bloom,
The grass is green, it's long and lush,
People relax more, life's not one big rush.
It's my favourite season, full of everything nice,
Paddling pools, ice creams, drinks full with ice.

Crystal Lane (10)

Summer Fun

The sun is shining, everyone's hot,
Some people are eating a lot.

It's wonderful weather
To see a bird's feather,
It's a beautiful day,
Don't waste it away.

I'll ride my bike
Because that's what I like,
Summer is here so have some fun,
Or just enjoy the lovely sun.

It's summer time,
Let's go to the beach
And have a splash
Because summer always goes in a flash.

Makalia Bobb (10)

Summertime

It is summertime,
Let's go to the beach,
The sun is shining
And the ocean is nice and cool.
Eat your ice cream like you don't even care,
Enjoy the gorgeous fresh air,
When you have done all the fun things you like to do,
Relax, lie on the sand and watch the sunset go down.

Elena Price (9)

Holiday Fun!

Yippy! Summer is here
I've got a lot planned,
Lying on the beach breezily fanned.
Look at the flowers!
What a pretty sight.
Kids, are you ready,
Have a water fight?
Fun, fun, fun in the sun,
Away from school,
No more homework,
Isn't that cool?
Now everybody smile
And let's hear you scream,
As we're finishing this summer
With chocolate ice cream!

Jay Kumra (9)

The Holiday

Holiday, holiday,
I went with my mum one day.
My belly started rumbling,
And Andre kept mumbling.
My mum started talking
And I started walking.

Eden Orianwo (8)

Holidays

I went to Australia,
but that was a failure.
I went to France
and did a dance.
I didn't like it there,
as it wasn't fair
because my brother said,
'I want the bigger bed.'
We finally made up our mind,
the place is one of a kind!
We went to Italy
because it was decorated prettily.

Italy!

Harriet Parsons (8)

The Friends

I may not be going on holiday
But I can still have fun.
I can have a great day
And have a great play and help everyone.
When someone's sad, lonely or lost,
I can help them out.
Summer is the best bit of the year,
It gets better and better,
Even though I miss our teacher,
Miss Macgregor!

Eloise Lynn (8)

The Swimming Pool

Chattering of the people,
Splashing of the waves,
Shouting of the children,
Laughing every day,
Boys on the board,
Hip hip hooray,
The screaming of the lifeguard,
'Get down and go away!'

People in the pool,
Splish, splash, splosh,
People on the slide,
Shouting, 'Oh my gosh!'
Sliding off of the floats,
People screaming, 'Argh!'
Cowboys coming in the pool,
Going, 'Ye ha!'

Emily Yarnold (10)

Summer Party

I am having a summer party
And I hope the weather is at its best.
I'm planning all of the games and fun,
Plus a gift for every guest.
And when it's over we will cry and cry,
When we realise that we must say goodbye.

Elle Baldwinson (10)

My Holidays

In the holidays, I'm going to Italy,
To stay in my apartment in Maccagno it will be.
I will go wakeboarding every day,
Surfing the waves, watch out for my spray!
Wakeboarding on my boat I will go,
It's the thing I'm looking forward to most you know!
And then there's the pool,
Jump in when it's sunny,
But when it is cold
It really isn't funny!
Mum lies on the sunbed
Going nice and brown,
When it gets too hot
She shops in the town.
After four weeks we will drive home once more,
Before you know it, I'll be in Year 4!

Georgia McConachie (8)

Hiding In The Dark

Things in the day, change in the night.
Shadows turn into spirits seeking revenge.
They moan from behind the radiator,
It's the werewolf screaming down the pipes.
The creak from upstairs is the puppet master's cold cackle.
The leak from the roof is the blood dripping from teeth of a vampire.
Thunder is a troll beating a colossal club.
Things in the day change at night,
Change in the night.
Watch out!

Charley Swire (9)

Summer Holidays

The sun is shining brightly while I'm having fun,
I'm playing in the park and the picnic has already gone!
I run around the garden, but not for very long
As I like to listen to the birds singing their beautiful song.
I go and ask my mum what this is all about,
Then I realise we're getting the paddling pool out!
I like to go to the beach and play in the sand,
The sun is beating down and we're all getting tanned!

When we go on holiday I like to go by plane,
When we get there, let's hope it doesn't rain!
The holidays are nearly over, we will have to go back to school,
But I will remember these holidays because they're really cool!

Alissia Brown (10)

My Summer Holiday

Summer holidays are supposed to be fun.
Well, not this one!
On the first night we stayed up late,
We watched Harry Potter until about 2:58.
Then, from the stairs we heard some sounds.
We hid behind the curtains and they all fell down.
Mum with an angry face was standing there,
She said if we did it again she would cut off our hair.
That was a key highlight of my summer.
I hope next summer will be much, much funner.

Abed Uddin (10)

Butlins

First we went swimming,
Then to 'Magic You Can Do',
Which is basically magic
That you can do too!
The big beach was really fun,
With giant towels and chairs,
It was like a great beach funfair!
Then I climbed the climbing wall,
But didn't reach the top.
I did a bit of archery,
But I couldn't hit the spot!
So that's what I did at Butlins,
Butlins in Skegness,
I really think Butlins
Is the very best!

Courtney Tanfield (9)

By The Sea

When I went to sit near the sea,
The waves came and splashed at me.

Then a dog came and threw sand at my toes,
I laughed and he froze!

Now I had to put my towel out,
Before that dog made me shout.

Then I had fish and chips for tea,
That was such a fun day for me!

Saira Khan (10)

My Summer Adventure

I went to Bridlington on holiday,
In the sea I did play.
The sea was very cold on that day
And then my teeth started to chatter away.

My mother shouted, 'Come back here,
I have got a towel, it's warm my dear.
We'll dry you off and get you home,
Just ready for an ice cream cone.'

And then the day was finally done,
I went to bed with a nice full tum.

Toni Barstow (10)

Warm Days In The Summer

Seagulls soaring in the air,
I can feel it on my hair.

Waves smashing on the rocks,
Crabs crawling on my socks.

Squashy sand on my toes,
The cool ice cream on my nose.

I could feel the weird sand,
At least I am on dry land.

Tiny spices on my chips,
So I started to lick my lips.

Mark Knight (9)

Sunset

The blazing colour covers the sky,
On the beach the beams flash by,
The clouds are glowing warm
Marigold, lemon, fuchsia and crimson.
Dancing shapes float around,
Sliding over the edge of the world.
The sky explodes with amazing colour
As the sun turns burning red.
Reflecting on the water
Shimmering on the gentle waves,
Shapes that are a blur,
As the sun sinks down below.
The sky flicks dark,
The light goes out,
The velvety darkness hangs down,
And night has fallen now,
On an idyllic holiday scene.

Katie Wheeler (10)

Untitled

When I go up mountains my legs ache.
There's a massive lake at the Lake District.
My holiday was laketastic!
The view was great and I loved what I ate.
I played rounders.
There were some funny fielders.

Elliot Tolman (8)

The Waves

Crash! Crash!
The waves
Frothing, foaming
Throwing little fishing boats
High and pushing them down
Deep down
Under the wild sea
Fight the storm
Tossing itself around
Crash! Crash!
Furious raindrops
Plummeted down,
Hurtling themselves
At the groaning waves
Crash! Crash!
I'm wrapped up
Against this wild holiday weather.

Bethany Baines (11)

Sunshine

The sun beams down
As the children play,
In the swaying grass,
As the wind blows past.

The sunshine's fading,
Time for bed,
Sleepy heads go to bed,
As the sun goes down
The moon comes out.

Cally-Jo Browning (10)

Fun!

It's either at home or your cousin's house,
Bring your best dress or your flowery blouse!
Go to your mate's place to play football,
Then find yourself playing with a bouncy ball.

You might be sea sick or afraid or heights,
It could be worse on very cold nights.
With your beach towel on the very hot sand,
You'll end up having a magenta red hand!

As you scream on the horrid ride of doom,
Your mother is sweeping with a long broom.
Up and down without making a leap,
Your dad is putting papers onto a huge heap.

Mariana Bongou (9)

Sun And Rain

The sun shined brightly now and again,
Then other times it was pouring rain!
When the sun shined we had so much fun,
Then the rain would come.
Even the rain can't dampen our spirits,
Because the sun still shines inside us.
Five months until Christmas,
Six weeks before school,
Whatever the weather,
It will be the best six weeks ever, ever, ever!

Esmee Martin (10)

So Much Fun

The summer sun,
The summer sun
Is so much fun
Or so I thought . . .

The sun blazing down
Burning me till I'm brown,
Waiting for the paddling pool
Thinking about being cool.
After my dinner
The paddling pool is the winner.

Finally at the end of the day,
The paddling pool is ready, hooray!

Eve Rowan (11)

Talking Trees

Trees sway side to side
Talking to each other
They talk in the sun
They talk in the rain
Never get bored of each other.

Trees are orange
Trees are green
There are quite a range to see
They'll never be seen
If you just sit inside and watch TV.

Imogen Harvey (11)

The Old Oak

It whispers to passers-by,
It dances in the wind,
Its branches reach up high,
For centuries there it's been.

It stands there proud and tall,
From the day that it was born,
Years before it shall fall,
Sat peacefully on the lawn.

Lea Walker (11)

Malta...

As the sun shines down
there's a smile on her face.
'Beautiful,' says he.
'Wonderful,' says she.
The wildlife is superb,
the houses are all clean.
'This is Malta,' says he.
So many memories to treasure,
so many things to tell.
'I hope we come back soon!' says he.

Holly Eckton (11)

One Boiling Summer's Day

Magnificent lifeguards saving children's lives,
Then all of a sudden I saw beehives.

My beautiful fish and chips,
So I can watch the ships.

My brother getting a suntan,
And I hear people cheering.

Running boys, having fun,
So come and have some!

Cameron Collier (9)

Beach

I collect sea shells,
One and then the other.
If it's windy I will fly my kite,
It goes this way and that.
I'll make a sandcastle with my sister,
And put a shell on the top.
We could play ball games as a family,
Volleyball or just throwing.
Then I will look for crabs and starfish.
I will sunbathe and chill out,
Just before we go I will listen to the shell,
It sounds like the sea,
Crashing and smashing.

Jade Brindle (10)

Lazy Summer Days

My feet in the soft sand
Excited days in the sun.

I could smell fish and chips in the air
My stomach begins to rumble.

Waves crashing into the rocks
Excited children everywhere.

Tiny crystals on my lips
And the lovely taste of the chips.

Joshua McHale-Shore (10)

Summer Holiday

Lazy days in the sun,
I like summer, it's just so fun.

'What's that noise?'
'Oh, it's the boys.'

I feel the sun beating on my chest,
I'm tired, I need a rest.

I love the feel of candyfloss melting on my tongue,
But there's nothing better than a summery song.

Jaime-Leigh Whitaker (10)

The Joyful Days Of Summer

The blazing sun in the sky,
Seeing all of the artefacts.

The lurking creatures in the ground,
The warm water clashing against me.

Hearing the cars going past,
Hearing the train coming along.

Tasting the bread which has been homemade,
Tasting the spices which are so hot.

I could taste the fresh air,
I could smell the wide open sea.

Matthew Callier (10)

Sunshine Summer

Sun shine on me, don't let the clouds go over me
If you do I will run to the sea
When I return you will see I will be mean as can be.
Now I belong to the sea, go and find someone just like me.
Just on my own, the sun is down, the sea is out
And I am sitting here all about.
Don't say no way, I will see you the next hot day.

Ellie-Jay Hall (9)

Summer Holiday

S corching scarlet sun
U nravel your happiness
M emories return
M arvellous sights
E njoy whilst you can
R aspberries and cream at the ready

H ot, hot, hot
O MG it's hot
L ying on the beach
I ce cream melting
D reaming by the sea
A zure blue sea
Y es I may have a suntan.

Sophie-Angela Irle (11)

Summer Holidays

Summer holidays are so much fun,
Out of all the holidays they are No. 1!
Splashing in the sea or rolling in the sand,
Somewhere near or in a distant land.
Close or far, hot or cold,
Summer holidays are always bold.
Playing with pets or chatting with friends,
Not things that drive you round the bend.
Wherever you are, whatever you do,
You won't want your holiday to be through!

Natasha Hansford (10)

A Poem From Florida

Shimmering lakes, glistening
The giant palms swaying in the breezy moonlight.
Red cardinals cautiously pecking at the bottle brush
Egrets grubbing around near the grass.
Alligators sunning themselves by the lagoons
Turtles swimming in the murky lakes
Waves crashing on the shore
Golfers playing in the distance
Shells sparkling in the sunshine
Alligators lurking in the mysterious lagoons
Grass swaying in the gentle breeze
Humidity tiring you out
Sun beating down on you.

William Slocombe (10)

My Summer Fun

The bright blue sky
The big yellow sun brightens the day up
You go down to the blue sultry sea
The dark yellow sand as you make a sandcastle
And the crabs come to your feet
The ice cream makes you cool
As it goes dripping down the cone making you all sticky
All the seagulls trying to steal the fish and chips.

Charlotte Baker & Rachel Jackson (10)

The Park

As I'm on the swing,
I start to sing.
As I glide down the slide,
I started to sigh.
As I was on the see-saw
My feet took off the floor.
As I was on the activity trail
I saw a snail.
As I was on the rocking horse,
I was thinking about the programme 'Inspector Morse'.
As I saw my sister on the baby swing
My phone began to ring.

Jade Brindle (10)

In The Sea I Could See

When I went to the sandy beaches
I looked at all the fishy creatures.
In the sea I could see . . .
A stinky, crazy, silly, catfish
Then I got a big lobster dish.
When I found some sticky gum
I went to go and see my mum.
Although I don't have any proof
But then the story just goes poof!
When I got into the car
I got a giant chocolate bar.

Erin Varney (9)

Wildlife

Wildlife's all around us,
It surrounds our precious world,
For everyone who's in it,
Its beauty's now unfurled,
Most animals are thriving,
But there's something in their way,
If we can help to stop it, then
They'll live another day,
From elephants to spiders,
They all deserve a chance,
If we can help to save them
Then the world will be enhanced,
Poaching's not the answer, it does no good at all,
If it all just continues then our world will slowly fall,
While that is all still happening
It's amazing that we own
Such an incredible selection
In our world and ours alone.

Dominik Jay Reynolds (11)

Summertime

S ummer is the time, we have six weeks of fun
U p in the plane to Spain for some sun
M e and my family playing in the pool
M unching ice creams, I'm totally cool
E veryone enjoying all the sights
R elaxing by day and partying by night.

Hannah Ballard (8)

My Holidays

It's the boring holidays,
I'm not having fun,
I'll be able to go and play,
When my illness has gone.
Yippee, yippee, it's Saturday,
There's now nothing the matter,
Today's the day I can come and play,
Because I'm completely better.
Aah, ooh, aah, it's Sunday,
I am so relaxed,
I will go to church today
And do more chillin' after that.
It's the end of the holidays,
I'm so excited,
In every single way,
And plus I am delighted.

Jayne Bird (9)

Life Story

When I was one I wasn't much fun.
When I was two I learnt how to chew
But when I was three I became more like me.
When I was four my mother shut my finger in a door.
As soon as I was five I learnt how to dive.
At the age of six I learnt many other tricks.
When I was seven I had my first holiday in Devon.

Emily Vernon (7)

Apple

Hanging from the tree,
Ruby red and shiny,
On a short stalk,
Fat and round,
It waves in the wind,
Then drops with a thump,
A nearby deer hesitates,
Then shyly takes a bite,
Savouring the fleshy inside,
Until it reaches the core,
Then gallops away,
Into the setting sun,
And I sigh,
At the miracle of nature,
That I have just seen.

Gemma Sneddon (11)

The Seaside

At the seaside
The sun is hot
Ice cream cools me down
I swim in the sea
And play in the sand a lot
Building sandcastles
For fun in the sun.

Ellie Cockerton (8)

Sunset

Slowly the blazing shape sinks into the land,
As it does its colour fills the sky.
From the beach you see it clear,
Orange, yellow, red and pink.
These colours, warm and comforting
Though still bright and eye catching.
The sky steadily explodes with colour
While the sun burns quietly.
Carefully the colour dies out
Then the skies change.
They change from a bright, lively atmosphere
To a calm, peaceful night.

Bethany Moore (10)

Summer Ride

I horse ride when the sun comes down,
The clatter of the hooves like thunder,
I don't go to town on rides
But to the forests wander.

The breathing of the horse is like a dragon's,
The foamy white sweat,
As the sun beats down,
As we ride into the trees
And leap the logs
Now behind me.

Stephanie Rymer (11)

The Seaside

Crash! Crash! Crash! go the waves,
The rocks are sharp and grey
Not safe to play.

Wa! Wa! Wa! goes my baby sister,
As the suncream is cold
On her tiny body.

Snore, snore, snore! goes my mum,
As she lays on the sand
Trying to get a tan.

Munch, munch, munch! I go
As I eat the nice picnic
Before Mum wakes up.

Caitlin Anna Mills (11)

Summer Days

S unglasses on and deckchairs out
U nder the sun, children are about
M ums tending flowers
M any outside for hours
E veryone's happy and jolly
R ainbow ice lolly.

Sophie Snow (8)

Mermaid Dreams

Just look at me,
Look at the sea,
As I jump into my fantasy!
Magical spirits of the deep,
I want a tail not two feet.
As I swim miles from land,
As I miss the coast of sand,
As I cry, when I sigh,
Where am I?
Mum, Dad, I miss you!
Help! Help! Lord save me!
Soon I arrived at sand, no more sea!
Thank you Lord for saving me.
As I look back at the sea,
Will you remember me?

Hollie Joice (8)

Untitled

The day was mottled with sunlight,
The winding path strewn with fallen leaves.
The overgrown shrubs protected every whisper,
The robin caressed her chick in her breast,
I yearned to know her lullaby,
Alas! She ain't let me near her.
Her resilience, I admire.
She is one of my teachers,
The more I learn, the more I grow.

Sriya Roy (10)

Summer Holiday

Summer will start with a beat of the heart.
Year 6 are gone but nothing's wrong.
Out of the gate, to see my fate.
My heart is a-beating,
My summer's completing.
Day by day, night by night,
And there's always a new sight.
In a new day, to the fair,
I go without a care.
Friday 13th, unlucky day,
I had something weird to say,
One day to September, that's the way,
My heart skipped a beat,
Because my summer's complete!

Sasha Hartwell (10)

Bikini Bottom

I have been to Bikini Bottom.
I saw SpongeBob and the gang.
Mr Krabs was counting his money.
Sandy was eating nuts coated in honey.

SpongeBob took me jellyfishing, it lasted all day.
I got a job at the Krusty Krab
Then I took a ride in a cab.
After that I saw Squidward in concert.

Faith Batchelor (10)

42 Days Of Fun

Summer, summer is so great,
You can go to bed too late.
Play all day in the sun,
Having lots of fun.
You can go to theme parks
And ride till dark.
One of my favourites is the zoo,
To see the monkeys have a poo
And the elephants too.
Splash, splash! in the pool,
Trying to be really cool.
Going on holiday is so fun,
Visiting foreign countries with lots of fun!
All too soon the holidays are over,
Going back to school
And forgetting all about the pool!

Ben Walker (7)

Summer Holiday

The summer sun has come so quick,
So you need to make your suncream thick.
Summer flowers are so colourful
And they are really wonderful.
Start to grow your summer's plants today,
Once they've grown say hooray.
Summer wildlife is so free,
If I were a bug I'd be full of glee.
I hope you have enjoyed this poem,
The sun's come out so I'm going.

Daniel Tunstall (9)

Summer

The sky is blue,
not a cloud to be seen.
The sun is shining,
like never before.
The grass is green,
not a shade of brown.
The birds are chirping,
singing their songs.
The trees are still,
not a slight bit of wind.
The flowers are beautiful,
blossoming like mad.
The bees pollinating,
one flower then the other.

Jade Brindle (10)

In The Summertime

Sun warm on my face
Cool breeze by the sea
Sand running through my fingers
Blue skies, cloudless day
Volleyball, fun and active
Picnic in the park
Underneath the cool leaves
Relieve my skin and breathe again.

Joshua Newton Taylor (8)

Summer Has Arrived

The sky is so blue, not a cloud in sight,
The Earth's painting every shade so bright,
Chirping birds sing, as they fly by,
Amidst the golden hue, of the open sky,
Its flowers are so fragrant, the trees are their shield,
For under the blistering heat,
It's the gentle summer breeze they should feel,
Voices of children playing near the park,
It's a definite sign that summer had made its mark,
The sea laps its gentle waves,
At the beach we do everything including visiting caves.

Mae Graham (10)

Fun In The Sun

S ummer holidays full of fun, this is what I did in my time
U nder the tree I played spot the bee
M e and my sister sang 'Mr Brightside'
M y mum went to work, I got a new skirt
E ars got pierced
R ead a book about deer

H yde Hall and the beach
O n Sunday I got sand in my feet
L ouise, my mum had lots of fun
I dip and dab in the paddling pool with my grandad
D id a flip in the sun
A nd had fun in the sun
Y ou just heard my summer holiday fun!

Imogen Ruth McBrearty (9)

Sleepover!

I got up at seven, had lunch at eleven
And Milly came round for a sleepover.
I waited till 4, she knocked on the door
And we had so much fun.
We had pizza for tea, it was so yummy
And this is my poem.
You would agree that pizzas are yummy,
You too would come round for tea.
We read a book, just had a look
And then we fell asleep.
In the morning Milly was still snoring for we were so sleepy.
The next day we went swimming, we had a race and Milly was winning!
We ate some bread rolls, then played with my dolls
Then Milly went home!

Arnya Robey (8)

Hawaii

Stepping off the plane,
The sun beats my brow,
I'm given a lei,
As well as a friendly bow,
I went to the beach,
And had a peach,
I went to the hotel
And brought back a shell.

Matthew Bryer (11)

In The Summertime

Water cool as it runs over my toes,
Shiny buttercups lay on the beautiful green grass,
The swimming pool's hot, water lying in the boiling sun,
Beautiful blue skies lay up above my head,
The warmth of the day is red hot.

Tennis and roses and so much more,
Sunbathe till cooler and take a bath,
Trees out my window, the sun is still hot,
I'll go and play volleyball, go on holiday or go for a picnic,
Till it's the end of the day.

Caitlin Amy Bell (8)

Sun Shining Bright

When I went to the seaside,
The sun was shining bright,
Just like the strongest light,
I think the sunbathing was the best,
Wearing my sunglasses and my best top vest,
The sand is tickling my toes,
And I am getting it on my nose,
Then I have an ice cream,
I woke up, it was a dream!

Abigail Barnes (8)

Holidays

Holidays, holidays
The time has come
Finally I have freedom
The beach, the beach
I've been here for ages
Luckily, it's coming out of my parents' wages
The caravan, the caravan
It's small, but cosy
It's definitely summer cos the bees are dozy
The discos, the discos
They're far from lame
With the funky groovin' and the odd bingo game
But now my story's all but done
A new school year has just begun
More sun, more sun
And a lot more chilling
Unfortunately it costs more than a shilling.

Bethan Breeze (10)

My Brother And I

Look at me,
I'm like the sea.
I'm a pop star.
My brother sings la, la, la.
We got an award, so whoopee!
That's the end of my poem.

Annalise Park (9)

Manor Adventure

Manor Adventure is the place I've been,
Climbing walls up and down,
Is something I've seen,
And the wood we climbed was brown.

Kayaking and canoeing is great,
I really enjoyed them all,
I was with my mate,
But I did have to crawl.

Breakfast, lunch and dinner were good,
It did rain a bit,
You did have to wear a jumper with a hood,
When it was time to do kayaking my face lit.

Ellie Hall (9)

In The Summertime

Sunny days brighten up my face,
Holidays are fun in the sun,
Going to the park is the best thing,
I make daisy necklaces in the breeze.

I have picnics in the sun, it is so fun,
My mum gets me dressed up for weddings,
I go swimming on holiday,
But it comes to an end as it is time for bed.

Amy-May Friend (9)

In The Summertime

Going on holiday to lovely places,
Eating strawberries and cream,
Having picnics in the park,
Splashing in the stream.

Tennis, badminton, fun and games,
Daisies, buttercups all coloured and bright,
Iced tea, cream tea, all different types,
Warm and also bright.

Ice cream, smoothies, yum, yum, yum,
Swimming in the sun,
Green leaves and trees,
Summer is fun!

Hannah Clifton (8)

In The Summertime

Sitting on the swings,
Having a picnic,
Mum calls me,
I wonder if there's an ice cream,
Staring at the flowers,
I think I might make a daisy chain,
We are on holiday, having fun,
Dad says we are having a barbecue,
Sitting in the swimming pool, having a nice bath.

Caitlin George (9)

Springtime

Springtime is the best time of year,
When all the birds come out and cheer,
You'll find the hedgehogs coming out to play,
But they'll just say go away,
Newborn lambs and daffodils,
Buds and tulips in the fields,
Swans and ducks swim across the lake,
When the farmer comes to rake.

The bees will shout and sting, sting, sting,
But the butterflies will just sing, sing, sing,
Spring, spring is so much fun,
I love dancing in the sun,
Newborn lambs and picnics too,
The blossom trees will sing to you,
Bunny rabbits jump so high,
They almost jump to touch the sky.

Lexie Elise Margetts (9)

Legoland

My dream holiday is to go to Legoland
And to play with real life Hero Factory Heroes
To get my driver's licence
Only if I was a millionaire
If I was I would go every day

I'd run around, going mad with joy
And obviously I'm a boy
Spilling my cash
I am so in love with Lego
I could wear a sash.

Timothy David Jeeves (10)

Untitled

The sun's out
Summer's come
Time for picnics
And lots of fun

Time for ice creams
In the heat
Whilst the sand
Tickles my feet

Long walks along
The golden sand
Then build a castle
Tall and grand

Or walk through
Forests with tall noble trees
As I sing
Happy melodies

Autumn's come
Summer's gone
Now let's sing
An autumn song.

Annabelle Marsden (11)

My Holiday Destination

M oroccan food was extremely hot
Y ummy, scrummy in my tummy.

H awaii hula skirts,
O dessa was very inviting.
L eeds football stadium was amazing.
I ndian dancers were very eye-catching.
D evon was hot,
A ustria was very cold.
Y oung tigers in Siberia.

D ublin, what a sight.
R ussia was tense, learning a new language.
E ritrea was very exciting.
A ustralia was as hot as anything.
M ali, so breathtaking.

Hayden Clamp (10)

In The Summertime

Sand is blowing between my feet,
The sea is flying as it is crashing on the dry sand,
Going up the park is fun,
In the sun, playing games on the grass,
Having picnics in the sun is really fun.

Swimming is so much fun
When you know how to have fun in the sun,
Using pistols in the sun is quite fun,
Eating ice cream in the summer is too much fun.

Hannah Bell (9)

The Best Holiday Ever!

Over the summer holidays,
I met Doctor Who,
He took me to the ancient world.

There were beasts here, there and everywhere,
With wings spread out wide,
The people knew they had to hunt,
But I decided to hide!

The Doctor gave me a tour,
And knocked on every door.

We met a giant bird twice,
And they both wanted a battle,
It wasn't very nice,
Because The Doctor covered it in lice!

George Cree (10)

My Trip To Tellytubbyland

My trip to Tellytubbyland,
I met my friends, they held my hand.
We skipped up the green hill then slipped back down.
As we looked at the baby-faced sun,
He smiled at everyone.
We strolled down to the dome
And had Tellytubby shaped toast.
Then when my trip was over
The rabbits came to say goodbye.

Georgia Clarke (10)

My Summer Holiday

I'm on my summer holidays,
These are the great days!
Even though I'm not abroad,
I do have a body board.

Across the sea I cannot go,
Because the price is not low.
The sea is not even warm,
Time for sun clothes to be worn.

Sunbathing on the beach,
Better not get bitten by a leech!
On my towel I shall lie,
Underneath the bright blue sky.

I don't want to get sunburnt,
That is one lesson I have learnt!
So, out of all I have seen
What have the best bits been?

Probably the swimming pool,
Not sitting on a stool.

Philippa Davies (10)

During The Holidays

During the holidays
I went away,
To Mars, to Jupiter,
The moon to play.

During the holidays
I went away,
Over the rainbow,
In Santa's sleigh.

During the holidays
I went away,
Down under the sea,
Fish swam away.

During the holidays
I went away,
To paraglide,
Move out of the way!

During the holidays
I went away,
To Candyland
To eat all day.

Georgia Warner (10)

Untitled

On my holidays I went to Cornwall,
I really like it there,
Our caravan is right next to the seaside,
And everyone will share.

Children playing in the sea,
Children playing in a pool.
Children just like me
And fish that are really cool.

Sand under your feet,
Burning in the sun.
Shells that are really neat,
You're having so much fun!

Lexi Jessop (10)

Comfortable, Cocktail Corfu

When I went to the island of Corfu
I got off the plane and said, 'Wah-hoo!'

I was in a lovely mood
For my really lovely food.

Vine leaves, pitta and so much more,
I ate so much I couldn't fit through the door!

I went to a beach in paradise,
Cooled myself down with a cocktail on ice.

The sun never went dim,
I loved to go for a swim.

Jacob Vidotto (10)

The Summer Of Paradise

Waves like horses, running to the shore,
And sand as bright as the sun,
Tropical fruits warming in the heat,
The sea glistens like stars in the sky.

The coconut trees reach out their leafy fingers,
Almost touching the ground,
Dolphins jump above the waves
And the waves give the dolphins a hug.
Sun, sea, sand is what the surfers see,
Jellyfish like a flat, squashed pancake
Washed up on the shore.

The usual fish and chip smell fills the air,
Seagulls as noisy as loud children.
The beach welcomes everyone,
If you want a fab holiday
Go to the Summer of Paradise!

Ria Becker (10)

Young Writers Information

We hope you have enjoyed reading this book - and that you will continue to enjoy it in the coming years.

If you like reading and writing poetry drop us a line, or give us a call, and we'll send you a free information pack.

Alternatively, if you would like to order further copies of this book or any of our other titles, then please give us a call or log onto our website at www.youngwriters.co.uk.

Young Writers Information
Remus House
Coltsfoot Drive
Peterborough
PE2 9BF

Tel: (01733) 890066
Fax: (01733) 313524

Email: info@youngwriters.co.uk